Lies *for* Morning

Collected Poems

Bob Gaskin

Lies for Morning
by Bob Gaskin

Copyright © 2024 Bob Gaskin

All rights reserved.

Printed in the United States of America
ISBN: 978-1-962802-24-6

All rights reserved. Except in the case of brief quotations embodied in critical articles and reviews, no portion of this book may be reproduced, stored in a retrieval system, or transmitted in any form or by any means—electronic, mechanical, photocopy, recording, scanning, or other—without prior written permission from the author.

High Bridge Books titles may be purchased in bulk for educational, business, fundraising, or sales promotional use. For information, please contact High Bridge Books via www.HighBridgeBooks.com/contact.

Published in Houston, Texas, by High Bridge Books.

"Of all lies, art is the least untrue."

—Flaubert to Louise Colet

Contents

Preface	xi
Section I	1
Bivouac in Never Wood	3
A Need for Ceremony	4
Single	5
Tacos after Reading Updike	7
Sundial	8
Father Fix-it's Nightmare	9
George	11
In Christine's Paris	12
Kathryn	13
David and the All Night Diner	14
After the Neighbor's Wedding	16
No Big Thing	17
In Another Country	18
Taxi-ing Past Mount Fuji	20
Museum Piece: 1956	21
Sea Story '57	23
East China Sea	23
Frisco, 2011	24

Section II   25
  Felix Culpa   27
  Sweeping Up Alone   28
  Browning Drive   29
  Chalk Horse   30
  Jim   31
  Thicker than Water   32
  Family Car   33
  Mortgage   34
  A Pejoration Against Twinhood   35
  Follow Me, Follow Me   36
  To Cousin Amanda in Heidelberg   37
  Ajar   38
  White Hills   39
  Family Man   40

Section III   43
  Maps, Flowers, Leaves and Weeds   45
  I Remember It Well   46
  After the Hurricane   47
  By Any Other Name   49
  Joyce   50
  The Fault with Green   51
  Thanksgiving Away   52
  Green Valentine   53
  Waiting on Boylston Street   54
  For Just a Day?   55

She	56
Look to a Wall	57
Fear and Lostness	58
Letter Poem for Joyce	59
Mnemosyne Shrugs	60
Attribution	61
On Your Gift of Gioia's Poetry	62
Before the Last Rejection	63
Section IV	65
Reading Our Letters, Last to First	67
They Said You Telephoned	68
Van Goes by Dairy Queen	70
Last Camp	71
Dysthymia	72
Träumerei	73
Devices	74
While I Wait	75
Last Paper Book, 2084	76
Used Readers	77
Western Ways	78
Insight Before a Slow Computer	79
Section V	81
The Custodians	83
Homage to Egil Scallagrimson	84
Thinking Low	86

The Bard	87
Wilfred Owen	88
Homage for Lieutenant Owen	89
Enigma	90
Looking for Work at Middle Age	91
From Chagall's Lovers in Venice	92
On Viewing De Andrea's Sculpture in Vienna	93
While You Were Away	94
Window Dressing	95
Figures of Speech	97
Substitute Teaching at Seventy	99
After Midnight Mass	100
Group Dynamics	101
Delmore	102

Section VI	103
Forces That Never Give In	105
Primal Sympathy	106
Hearing the Language	108
Tsunami	109
Peacocks	110
Lunchbox Gen	111
Spring Planting	112
Amateur	113
To Dirt Returneth	114
Earthquake	116
Nightmare	117

April's Way	118
Art and Its Place	119
Pour Me Another	120
Prayer Patch for an Octogenarian	121
Section VII	123
Sparrow Psalm	125
Wonder	126
After the Ovens and Palaces	127
In a Holy Rain	128
Better Things to Do	129
Die Eiserne Jungfrau	130
Moses from the High Ground	131
Fantasia for Maundy Thursday	132
Alypius in the Coliseum	133
Dust and Ashes	134
Absurd	135
Creation	136
Todesangst	137
Don't Ask	138
Cold Island	139
The Door	140
Section VIII	141
Lies and Paper Angles	143
Night and Day	144
Gerade Aus	145

Art's Weakness	146
Letter To My Kinder	147
After a Friend's Posthumous Anniversary	148
Midnight Ghosts	149
Go Your Way and Tell No One	150
Last Words	151
Deliver Thee From Evil	152
My Place	153
Last Whole Earth Song	154
And Now to Close . . .	155

Preface

MY HUSBAND, BOB GASKIN (1933–2024), WROTE poetry most of his adult life, from around 1959 until 2022. Approximately 75 of his poems were published in small journals, such as *Concho River Review*, *Pulse*, and *New Mexico Humanities Review*. Two were published in national anthologies and one in *First Things*, a Catholic quarterly. He was the review editor for *Cedar Rock* from 1980 to 1984, and he also had reviews in other notable publications. For decades, Bob considered collecting his poems into a book. Early on, he found the Gustave Flaubert passage from which he created the title for his collection, *Lies for Morning*.

Bob had a wide range of interests, one of them being his love of the German language. Once asked why he chose German as his second language, he responded that as a child he had seen a movie in which there were lines of German spoken and that he fell in love with the beauty of the language. On the first page of a journal he kept was the following quote:

> *Der Schmerz ist ein heileger Engel, und durch ihn*
> *Menschen grosser geworder als durch alle Freuden der Welt.*
> (Pain is a holy angel, and people have become greater
> through it than through all the pleasures in the world.)[1]

Bob's poems express the beauty, the fear, the irony in his world woven by this "holy angel of pain."

Some of his personal poems reflect this expression, as in the poems he wrote at the deaths of two close poet friends—George de

---

[1] 1859. Adalbert Stifter, Austrian novelist and painter.

Schweinitz and David Yates. One was old and died of cancer; the other was young and died by suicide. In these poems, he employed aesthetic distance in expressing sensitivity without avoiding reality, as he did in the poems about his divorce in "A Need for Ceremony" and "Bivouac in Never Wood." In the latter, the persona views his own guilt in light of paths once intended but not taken. Bob's sensitivity extended to animals, too, as in "Hearing the Language," which presents the harsh death of a crushed animal.

War was a part of Bob's growing up years, and he had a scholarly fascination with World War II, especially with the resistance movement. Dietrich Bonhoeffer and Sophie Scholl (one was hanged and the other beheaded by the Nazis) feature in several poems, often dropped in only by first names. In "Better Things to Do," Bob contrasts classic Germany with the depravity of the Third Reich. He admired Wilfred Owen's World War I poetry, which looked at the hideous reality of war stripped of any romantic ideals. "In a Holy Rain" compares the beauty of Schiller and Mahler to "shattered ceilings" and "distant planes," ending with the offhand remark that Dietrich preached here once, "but, of course, we didn't hear him."

Bob had a deep interest in the arts, as well as in clever, sardonic humor, evidenced by his master's thesis, "Wit in Walpole's Letters," a study of the eighteenth-century writer and art historian Horace Walpole. In poems such as "Homage to Egil Skallagrímsson," his wit treats layers of power and greed which craft the persona's image of the barbaric Viking storyteller and begs the difference. Sometimes, as in "Some Forces Never Give In," the humor is whimsical but delves into other levels and eras. More dry humor comes with "The Custodians," those who senselessly ruin beauty and meaning in art. "They season now the porridge just any way they please."

His poem titles skillfully do what titles should do—explain and reveal. "Van Goes by Dairy Queen" plays on words in an obvious way. "Lies and Paper Angles" studies the birth of a child's lie with the mastery of cutting angles with scissors.

Bob Gaskin

There is music in Bob's poems, and in recognition of that, his grandson, Samuel Gaskin—an organist of international reputation—set his grandfather's poem, "To End By," to music and presented the piece in concert, with Samuel on organ and opera soloist Jacquelyn Matava singing the words.

Bob was a quiet poet, but he relished appreciation of his work. All his poems are worthy of careful reading.

—Joyce Gaskin

Section I

Bivouac in Never Wood

The weather-blasted trail marker whispers
its *Never*, its only just legible word.
A warning sign? Bad water? Surely not bears
this high, possibly alpine flowers once.
All that seems special now is the view down.
You can prove how high you came.

A boot print is enough to tell that hikers
paused here days ago. Perhaps comet watchers,
there's a good sky west? No, I scorned its
silent shouldering by, errant among the stars,
ice ball, thespian, all plumage in
the highlight of its vacuum.

But meteors? I lie, watching through the mesh
the brave end of light years.
What if she's out on an evening walk?
What if she saw that one?

I dream the ragged sign has lost its "N."
We are on an outing, to some lake or park,
all in the blue Ford, our ordinary family.
We stop by McDonald's again.
I hold McDonald's door for them.
I had never broken their trust. Never wood.

A Need for Ceremony

Some manner of ceremony
could begin now, your ring
brought in on a pillow,
and I to pull a bell
for clarions, some flourish worthy
of terminus so momentous.
The boxed books
silent in a cone of light.

Perhaps I now should sigh, you shrug,
don those masks we couldn't burn
one last time. Match,
if we can, dear Dali and Proust.
Part on affectations we have learned.

We could have brewed this cinematically,
a few leaves of the story of never-was,
have what began in a frame parsonage
seem to end at Saint Paul's.

But it hurts, listening for the scalk
of hooves and carriage rims on stone.
The knights we had have dipped their capes
and gracefully withdrawn. Hamlet,
Ophelia, rise. The curtain, dears, is down.

Single

I look out the kitchen window
to see which way the dogs
are barking. To see
where the postman is,
knowing it's the wrong time
of the month for meter readers,
the wrong season for linemen
who come in summer
to trim the limbs. Kind of
knowing dogs and how
they bark in chorus
when the postman passes
or in frantic arias
when someone breaches backyard fences.
This takes time to learn.

I walk out the rented door
into the rented yard
that someone else will mow,
free, free of that worry,
to watch the evening through
someone else's pines.

I think neither of us were pretty.
The day would end with mirrors
eavesdropping on failure and the city
sound of ambulances in the night.
We slept in other decades,

cheaper rooms. The bathroom light
cast its lean yellow on platoons
of cordbare carpeting...

Tacos After Reading Updike

She gave me my order
with such dignity as she could
pushing two crispy tacos across to me.
Silently, I said, "You're so beautiful.
It's almost a sin to be you."
But, of course, one doesn't.

From just under her left ear,
a large tattooed name, a boy's,
curved around her neck to the midline
of her throat. I imagined the artist's hand
and perhaps the blitzed boyfriend.

What if now she no longer cared for him?
Does some new kid kiss her neck,
wishing his ardor could erase
the skin-deep promise of fidelity?
Could he bed and wake to such daily irony?

As I munch, the thought haunts even me.
I recall the grandiose promissory inky loops
on a first marriage license, once on a wall,
now filed deeply away among invalid guarantees,
big box receipts, and out-of-date repair guides.
And wonder that she keeps my name?

Sundial

Now the sun is half down in the western trees,
having double-traversed heaven
since you left last morning,
lifting its light the millionth time
off men's affairs.
Shadows return on spider's knees
like pilgrims eastward, past
the tousled ruin of your bed.

Father Fix-It's Nightmare

for George de Schweinitz

Tonight, the dishwasher slows to a waterless grind.
Last weekend, the clothes dryer quit,
And a headlight went out on the Toyota.
Last night, I learned my old friend had cancer bad.

Tonight, I go to the hospital. The Rockets are on.
But for an occasional nurse, we are alone.
We got through the strike like this, working
Poems, listening to Mahler, and drinking wine.
I'm relieved he's not terrified, as I would be.
We speak some of the disease. I recall
Those I know who had it and still lived,
Joyce's mother, old man Ben, myself.
I can't tell him I'm still scared.

I say I found this book for Hugo in Missoula
Just right for him—someday. I'll bring Miller's
Autobiography. They found it in the colon, too,
He says, and aren't done looking.
James Wright, yes. He has two of his for me.
After an hour, I leave, the Rockets down by six.

I tinker some more, and the washer gushes to life

Lies *for* Morning

In surges and sprays. A plastic spoon had fouled
A float valve. Joyce cheers and says I have the touch.
I could fake it at Lourdes for pots and pans.

George walked on sticks and opened doors
I couldn't get through on my own. I doze.
The washer hums a hymn for sodden floors.

George

The hospital sent us home with an aluminum walker.
I'm learning, but it is harder than you think.
I've bucked off it once onto the driveway;
Trimmed by the simple lawn I was trimming
One doesn't lift oneself out of here. I need the Kleenex.
But it sits across the hall in the kitchen by the tub
Of sweets Melanie brought, under a plastic balloon of
Happy slogans: "Way to go," "Look at you," "What a job?"

Time's irony wash-paints a hippie-less wall now.
Snot runs down my moustache. I manage the walker nearer
my armchair. No one around to hear me struggling
to get upright squarely in the walker. Oh, but he's here.
George smiles approvingly from an old desk photo.
"Now you see?" "Get it now, old man?"

In Christine's Paris

Settled on the bus, the tour group watched us leave,
young you, ancient me, we two to a Metro Station.
"Well! This is Paris," Joyce heard one woman say.

Is this not the way a proper film noir might begin?
Except it was I, not Grant, not Bogart, or Kevin Kline,
but I on the *Arc de Triomphe* you made me climb.

We could see the *Bois de Boulogne* where Rubirosa
died, pants on and all. On the distant hill of *Sacré Cœur*
and down the steps into Montmartre, I'm half Hemingway,

casing Henri de Toulouse's windmill, then to Hugo's Notre Dame
and Joyce. With her and you, Christine, we three
by a low sun in Paris. Who could ask me what I saw?

In the story I would tell, the guide would say, "Insurance,
you understand. She can't come." I would have to choose:
Go on the bus, pass Napoleon's tomb, the tower, the Seine.

Or walk around Paris with Christine.

Kathryn

There is an unfinished poem for you
that I might have sent
but, being myself, did not.
You'd have liked it, faults and all,
as you did me and other undeserving ones.
But no, you died in your sleep last night.
That was so like you. Now I am left
to wonder what I might have said
if I had said what I didn't say.

David and the All-Night Diner

for David Yates

It's boring now the all-night diner is closed.
My desk is a skyline of serious stuff
to read. My marriage died of fidelity to it.
After you were dead,
they called you tender-hearted;
their heart was in the right place.

Two poems of mine made it from the diner
to national anthologies. I know, I know,
specialists might say that's not serious.
They're probably right.

Half your problem was you had no cynicism
and kept promises you made drunk
and published things you soberly dreaded.
Half your problem was art wasn't always first.
And yet, you said between drinks,
"Poetry is my life,
know what I mean." Seriously.

Bob Gaskin

I just put down an article that says
"serious poetry" half a dozen times.
My desk is a skyline of serious stuff
to read.

Chuck and I talk.
Did you know part of the pain of
prison is it's a childless world?
Spring is going away.

I still have the menu, Dave.
Only black coffee now. I only eat
where they keep it coming.
The order can take forever for all I care.

After the Neighbor's Wedding

He, bowlegged and Polish in his tux,
Who measured his life by hours worked,
And nothing came by luck;
He of the graying crew cut
Gave his blue-eyed girl away
As easy as nailing down a loosened shingle.

The couple drove off into a rain-washed sunset.
An elder widow wept at one more impossible dream.
Husbands huddled to watch one end.
Ali finished, covering his chin.

Into his attic-stashed Jim Beam,
He opens the chain fence for the dog.
The dog marks his sure post. Pavlovich laughs.
He knows pissing in the wind.

The better half thumbs through her shoebox
Of photos: the new-used '58 Chevy,
The dawn after their first night in Galveston,
The day she cut her cascading hair
Six inches too short for him.

No Big Thing

That boom is the East China Sea coming over
The fo'c'sle. Son, it's no big thing. See now,
She shivers like a fish when the fantail clears.
The helm can hold her, however rough the sea.
    Sailors don't care, Juan would say

Like when you're old and nothing seems stable again,
Or in a Frisco quake and benchmarks move,
And level ground rolls in sea swells,
You walk the weather, but carry on.
    Sailors don't care, Juan would say

And when the blinds slap your land window,
And cups tinkle like Christmas in their racks,
You think it's your drunken father through the wall,
Wild as Poseidon wading ashore again.
    Sailors don't care, Juan had said

Son, the earth slips to no intention.
The great fault moves is all.

In Another Country

At taps, I look upon a bay filled with dark ships.
They came in at night off the Sea of Japan,
carriers, destroyers, frigates, etc., etc.
Someone closed a canal in the Middle East,
and we get ready for war.

Over the heavy surface of the bay,
a shipboard bugle blows,
and then a chaplain prays a war prayer.
Among the moored ships, his disembodied voice flows;
he speaks of faith and death and Caesar's due,
of proper-preparedness and sleep,
and closes on the Prince of Peace.
My eyelids grow as heavy as the water.

I think everyone was impressed:
the drama, the silhouette of a mountain
stooped like some ancient god
dragging a hopeless burden on his back,
the blue lights dotting the bay
like a Japanese Christmas tree,
and the surf's faint moan, coming,
going, like a drug-dream, when the wind turns —
something that needs deciphering —
a fisherman holding a lamp to his sail,

Bob Gaskin

or salmon dying on rocks
or leaping upstream again,
or blind eels lolling in bottom mud
like leftover beginnings.

Taxi-ing Past Mount Fuji

As if God had spilled his ice cream cone
    Strawberry in the late sun
    Of January Fuji stood
Like a cone in a candy maker's wood
    Old Sol in ices and lapidary.

We were told a spirit keeps the heights
But since a weather station is up there
    I doubted if it were true
Or that he's moved its metric scrolls a hair
"Like the yeti-lore of Katmandu" I smiled

As we sped on toward the Ginza's garish lights
Knowing more of spirits than pagan cabmen do.

Museum Piece: 1956

Hand bones in a ball of rough glass.
Nagasaki. A man drinking beer.
The flash. Less than a second
to the melting point of glass.
Metacarpals like mustard seed in plastic.
Slight errors of setting aside,
the stopped clocks all agreed.

I sip my beer in a quiet bar. Nagasaki.
Near the Cathedral of Saint Francis Xavier,
whose final mass unflyable clouds condemned.
Women mostly. Children, invalid men.
A fractured torso of the redeemer
stands against the blown-down portico.

Someone should write it,
how the cornucopia turned back its fruit to God
or nirvana or to another realm
that believers could tell about,
an ode for children trailing sparkling clouds,
backing away from the world.
Nun haben wir besseres, besseres zu tun.

The chaplain tabulates his cases
of drunks, VD, and body lice,
damning the spirochete and potable alcohol.
He invokes an abstemious Paraclete.
Some sign cards by way of pledge.

Lies *for* Morning

Tonight, let truth stow its abstract lash.
Do your gift, describe
the green-twig taste of the beer's
guaranteed consecration.
Note the wooden floor and the way
angled shadows move
in the receding light, subtle,
like the prints of human feet
through otherwise trackless ash.

Sea Story '57
East China Sea

A night smoke by the lifeline,
flat sea and slow roll.
Plankton foam out from the hull.
I surmise that if they thought,
they'd think their sea
had no shore. I'm sure that we
will reach Hong Kong in a week.

Far less might they imagine me
immersed in a kind of why
teachers would call teleology.
I flick a butt into forever
and follow the night lamps
down to sleep…

Frisco, 2011

From shore at Fort Point, the bridge is foreshortened.
A tourist noted how photographs made it seem larger.
In '57, from the deck of a navy ship steaming under,
I watch its immensity pass overhead.
Still, everything seemed bigger then.

Then I, true living's *tabula rasa*, had scarce begun,
conscripted from Junker Elementary on.
The Greyhounds grind east from here, back across
the steppes. But Frisco is truer from the open sea.
Off to port is Alcatraz. Would they be watching us?

Tourists pay to go there now. Cruise ships and yachts
whitewash the piers, and you can pick your "town,"
China, gay Castro, aged hippiedom, sociological Haight,
in enameled, kitschy boxes of cartoon-cultured paradox.
Places one can deviate to alone, even call it home.

Section II

Felix Culpa

No, the problem is in you. You should
never watch him in such a play.
You, huddled back seat to see your son
play a drunk! He doesn't mean it, but
he mocks us to the bone; deserved,
of course, if you've been a father
and a drunk. His lines were writ in chalk
no soft eraser will remove. In you, too.
You can't abide his eyes in such a light,
his chopped speech, even less the way
his drunk struggles to affect sobriety.
You wince at the comedy they find in that.
The audience roars at us.

Sweeping Up Alone

This morning, sweeping the kitchen floor,
I found a lock of my daughter's hair,
some strands that escaped the broom
after I trimmed it for her last evening.
I picked them up, and with my lips
I kissed the golden strands of hair,
then dropped them gently into the dustbin,
just as someone, someday, will lay
my darling in her tomb.

Mortar for a field mouse's home,
her hair will lie among cabbage leaves,
old auto rims and bones
this time tomorrow afternoon.
I think it's time to put more coffee on.

A cardinal flies past the patio door,
red margin on a page of green.
The telephone rings. Lakefront lots.
A voice sniffs, then begins to explain
the benisons of solitude.

Browning Drive

for Malcolm

I walked through again before it sold,
the house I can almost image I built.
And it was forty-five years ago,
and we were checking its wonders.

Then our youngest found himself shut out
the patio door, and he was screaming
as if he thought we might have left. No,
it wasn't funny then, even less so now.

I fumbled open the odd but simple latch,
hurrying as if he were struggling for air.
Knowing what that kind of fear can do.
Full of the simple power to hug him in.

Chalk Horse

We'd never known nor even seen our half-brother.
We knew the chalk carnival prize he had sent
was Mom's treasure. To us, it was an ill-placed
familial tackiness in motley mossy green, boned within
by twisted wires. Hence, it survived its accidents,
often fractures, always by one of us—a crippling
by pastern, by ear, by hoof, to its flowing tail.
As youngsters roughhousing, we would bump it.
Then scatter to hide, puzzling how our otherwise
artful mother so silently wept, setting back
that final swirl of woven wire and chalk.

Still, do we not see pieces as simple in fine museums:
bent beams, cones, tubes, and photographed
lightning strikes, whose thunder only the artist heard?
Some as vague as Sophie's summer blouse.
Notice how patrons circle otherwise refuse:
canisters emptied of their pesticides,
slabs of graffiti-ed walls. How docents guard
the way a seashell holds its grief.

Jim

I watched Jim, my beloved brother-in-law,
carefully table-folding towels and napkins.
It took a watch to stop him. Why
would he in his Alzheimer's do that?
In his own hospital room? For whom,
with us around? What else could he do,
having lost our names? What other
disorder gloomed the room of this
delightful, joyous man? Folding,
napkins and towels lay at hand.

Thicker than Water

In real-time, I watch the shower water run.
Does it flow clockwise as they said
or carry away sin, as one kind dreamer claimed?
Had Uncle's blood swirled like this down an autopsy drain?
Father said, "They keep some for evidence."

At ten, I didn't get how a chaser
after whiskey causes a gag response
or how the alveoli shut down,
but I heard the growls and chokes
and covered my ears and couldn't scream.

I still see the shadows and the son, and father,
the forlorn intervener, carrying his dying brother out.
Funny how things hang on past all counsel:

"Go cheer someone, someone worse off.
What you have figures in some." Huh?
The shower door locked and the water on warm
last door down from the family room,

>   *You left your doll in the rain.*
>   *How stupid is it to cry*
>   *for a melted paper face*
>   *you could never see again?*

Family Car

Motorcycle officers escort us through the lights.
Private introspection fills the immaculate car.
Being escorted dignifies the inner silence; all is inference,
the toting up of kindnesses and passing lonely windows;
doors we slammed, meals we might have shared.
Much is better left unsaid.

Weather offers a topic. Over there's
the plot where a witty uncle lay. And he?
We've a lock of his baby hair in a folded envelope,
skip how we brushed insects off his face.
Mum about the body bag. Let the leaves
we bore him through have their say.

Mortgage

You wish there were a magic
Rewind to time's arrow,
Only a temporal reverse,
Say five minutes worth
Or even an hour. If only you
Could have said goodbye,

If you of languages could
have heard your garbled name,
in the sound they were trying
to imitate, instead of frying
midnight eggs. Just one
line of thought too late.

"Try giving her something to drink,"
We said one day of a down horse.
Time to listen to a cold chest
Before the insects came. Perhaps,
You could have kept them away.
Like a sailor looking up at a star
That hasn't moved in light-years

A Pejoration Against Twinhood

Twins. That's no way to be born,
to play out your childhood as half
a corny novelty act.
No one needs an equal partner
at his birth, and every birthday
thereafter. And who
needs just half the hugs,
more or less?

Why couldn't I have been, say, left-handed,
instead of a left person?
And twin jokes! It's worse
than having a pun-prone name.
You've heard them all before you're six:
"Is your name Pete or Repeat,"
"Do you look in the mirror
and think you see your brother?"
Minnesota: may their scores be ever halved.

One day, for a joke, Dad said
the hospital crossed our names at birth
and I was really my brother.
What was funny was, at that age, see,
I really wasn't sure I was me.
Isn't that a scream? Like in that old cartoon
where Casper walks through snow
and leaves no tracks. And everybody laughs.

Follow Me, Follow Me

What special dread now lurks Alzheimer's?
My brother can't handle passwords or dial a phone.
Numbers kept names, not so sequential order.
Ideas of right and wrong are balanced as smoke.
Refutations are angering, reasoned or not.

My twin brother said my son steals from him.
An absolute error, his sound mind would know
It couldn't be. Yet now he wordlessly
Opens his door for me to leave his lostness.
Our identicalness begs its obvious question.

To Cousin Amanda in Heidelberg

May these flutings from my tinny pipe
Amuse you and earn your smiles,
But remember that apples plucked unripe
The eater's dream defiles.

So save these for some tedious road
And take them out at leisure,
And read how like a spastic toad
Is your poor poet's measure.

And then perhaps the miles will be
Shorter and less staid,
And you might, smiling, think of me,
And I will be repaid.

Ajar

for Anna

Flashbacks of the thirties
crossed on the morning wind.
Ghosts of quiet perfume,
scents of a '30s stove,
burled firewood,
and tub-washed clothes.
The true faith smell
of a baby's head.
Cleaner than clean,
than the new sedan
I sat a minute in.

White Hills

A gimpy knee got me around the mall
as far as the "Lone Sailor." He's gazing off
as sailors will, say waiting for a ship.
But wouldn't it already be in port?
The after-gangway down, his sea bag,
too heavy, waiting for his shoulder?
It's gospel, lateness, for him, is no problem.
Possibly, somewhere has botched a schedule.
Even an important one, remember Tarawa.

Joyce, my legal bond to honor's claim,
went down Tuesday, or was it the day before,
to rub her cousin's name off the Wall.
Just yesterday we watched full-dress marines
bury his father near him across the river,
with his seventy-three-year-old Navy Cross.
I stood as a sailor at the slow-played hymn,
as if it were Tarawa or Vietnam or peaceful,
loving Sasebo or up here far from home.

Family Man

For Maxie R. Williams Col. USMC
Arlington National Cemetery, Spring 2011

Drafted in, I was once a white-hat sailor.
To us, you would call everybody "sir,"
even the marine detail hefting his coffin
from the caisson to the open ground
and certainly to the colonel, the Navy Cross
on his blue tunic, fit for that heavenly guard.

And I, who was only a white-hat sailor,
touched my ancient dog tags to his coffin,
its simple navy gray metal, the flag folded
and removed, the chaplain done. Miss Jean
commended in the name of the President of the United States
and the commandant of the Marine Corps.

The colonel's son, a marine lieutenant, already lay
A few steps up the hill; same name but for "junior" here and
across the river on the Wall, within the nightly glow
of Lincoln's holy tomb. A black ranger took our picture there.
After the colonel's funeral, Joyce went back for another rubbing
but only could get the name. "Jr." just would not print this time.

Bob Gaskin

As I walked behind the caisson that they carried him on,
the drum cadence and the hymn and hoof-claps on the road,
echoes deep and honor bound told an old story
of a way I wish I had been better at, yet proud of the grace
of our family who welcomed me in, an officer's country
of the heart, a white-hat sailor among marines.

Section III

Maps, Flowers, Leaves, and Weeds

They trade these old books with scarce a flip,
Some autographed, some lovingly signed.
Most have been isolated. You know when a book
Has been truly used; there's smell, scruff of attics,
Garages, closets, some abandoned under leaky
Backyard roofs. You guess a humane history by the skin.

Trust the opened book to tell you more, the endpaper
Rhythms of forgetfulness: her scent that night now long ago,
The wind's soft moving of the weather door, the moonlight's
   matrix
On the carpet, the fan he made with her soft hair.
Inside you find a faded sunflower, you think a field's soft scent,
You lift it out and wonder. Or here's a linden leaf,
There a weed that bloomed in secret memory once.

On our shop wall, I pin a desiccated flower
On our giant map of London. I guess the place
Where Shakespeare's Hermia woke to love a dunce
in Regent's Park one night, ten walking minutes from our room,
torn tickets tucked just for us, in our still precious book.

I Remember It Well

"As poets so often do, he required his muse,"
guide Sabrina said, under a stone Goethe.
"Yet he was always faithful to his wife."
I betrayed no doubt, as if he had been
my foghorn on a rock, a mast itself
for a rowdy crew. Our ever near
Mephistophelian Fiend in irons below.

As Sabrina droned on, I thought of you,
more than thought, in Neches-bordered Beaumont:

> *You, holding a lighted candle end*
> *close, over a wad of my pages,*
> *letting its warmth drip and seal.*
> *Lifting the candle then for me to snuff,*
> *knowing I will, with finger and thumb,*
> *slowly so the fingers burn.*

O why? What boots the muddy Danube near?
O why am I here, my poem?

After the Hurricane

for Joyce

"...*spirit, must it lodge in shrines so frail?*"
—Wordsworth, *Prelude, Book Five*

As if a rapture had passed in the night,
graves lay opened; caskets of gas and air
floated up to an unmasked no-man's land
once leveled by closing prayer and backhoes.
A pause for anyone who made love
in a cemetery; a nod to promises, feeling's
depths, to truths implied, and to the iron
Eternal Rest hanging from its post.

Shouldn't we accept that we are dust
with scant need to walk again,
closer to a cloud than to a human?
In urn or columbarium, at home
or scattered, say, on an indifferent sea,
borne like a child, past all corruption?

Lies *for* Morning

Dear, the deciduous leaves are down.
Step lightly. As if this were our aisle:
in passing they've sprinkled the mud
with brief vermilions, yellows, and rusts,
soft like bedding against the berm.
Mnemosyne's dropped handkerchief.

By Any Other Name

for Joyce in Her Absence

This must have been how Mendeleev felt
identifying the elements, arranging, classifying;
in his brilliant ignorance, leaving blanks
where something had to fit, helium,
germanium, which others would identify.

Thus may we see one day faith's ignorance,
like love that Jung could never define,
or costly kindnesses Freud could not explain.
The way the sun washing leaves outside my window
seems to beg your name.

Joyce

If you should pass on before me,
I would keep in your Book of God
The leathery creases and buffs
to remember you by, for you too roughly
held it at times. But held it you did.

As I do cherish the sun lines in your face
and keep for myself the sacred beauty
that others cannot see. You were God's gift
for me. This side of His glass, the shadows fall.
Your memory whispers me what I am.

The Fault with Green

for Joyce

Roses are red, violets are blue.
Rest assured, this much is true.
But soon the flower's rosy red
sinks like ashes to its bed,
just as the violet's noisy bright
lies dead in the prom floor's empty night.
But I can make (I too will die)
a better flower for your eye,
a poem to wear its paper page
through our gardens' rot and age.
A leaf for you that every year
says my darling touched me here.

Thanksgiving Away

for Joyce

Twenty-four years. Our first Thanksgiving apart.
A problem if it were not
that love crosses borders unimpeded
by concertina wire,
passports, even armed guards.
Hands through boarded prison windows
have spoken dear names, hands of the doomed
who could never touch again,
lovers unseen
across a scrabble road two stories down.

Love mocks deadlines, smiles
at death's attempt to cancel it.
Let scythes swing as ever they will
where flowers grow. Or where my pillow is,
as miles away you know.

Green Valentine

Green is your color, better then these cards of red,
a color-rhyme to the scent of your baking bread
and memories of mountains, quiet fires, and times
we secretly shared, written in our half-wise minds.
I shun these blossoms dull by tomorrow noon
and leave my poem, lost in bright leaves of green,
a Joyce poem, green for you, for you alone.

Waiting on Boylston Street

I knew that you, as you pass, would look for me,
puffing up that hill in Newton Mass, your sixth
denial of legend's claim. I see you seeing me
at the crest of Heartbreak Hill. I have made it
back to Boston, and then upstream by train
through the lead packs escort's lights and sirens.
How often through old man's glasses, hungry, knowing
Vigil for your projected time. From this seat, I watched,
knowing names, as the best in the world glide past.

To Heartbreak in time, I see my own personal best,
your paintless, ruddy face sweating up a cold hill.
You'd remember me, leaping, shouting from the berm.
Five miles more until you pass the Citgo sign. Then
another mile, and you turn in on Boylston Street.
You don't ask Wyeth's Helga what she is thinking.
Nor do I ask you, deep breathing, huggable you.
Tonight, we will be us again.

For Just a Day?

for our anniversary

For a day? A rock musician?
Fifty thousand howling as I wail?
Husband of a diva? Or just once,
bowl a perfect game. Or do it
with golf clubs, sink a forty-footer
past the camber of two hills.
Naw. That you would love me, and I you.
Have that to keep. But that is every day.

She

She opens her chemise and hugs your hurt.
Watches her flowers open to the sun. More than that,
Exclaims, "How beautiful." You half believe they know
She loves them. She of the raisers of the ordinary
Into better stations, of the appraisers of the lated sky's
Mockery of us, of our de Koonings, Pollacks, and Miros.
Who unto a sunset says, "How beautiful is now."
Oh could it not be she, after life's long lavings,
Past a poor poet's dreaming, opens God's great door
Forever and out of time to take me in.

Look to a Wall

for Joyce

My waking anxiety, I suddenly
realize this morning is like a
child's fear of abandonment, pure fear
of being "left" at school surrounded by
strangers. It takes some "getting over."

I put on my nearby clothes, lie
back down a bit, do some little chore,
avoid self-abandonment to
pointlessness, out of lostness.
Age's ending future? God would

help. You must have faith.
School fear haunts a teacher
on old mornings, *Phi Kappa Phi*
hanging on a wall.

Fear and Lostness

for Joyce

Walk past sight of the last snow wand,
spin around,
look for the guesswork sun,
flooded by where you've come.

Say, in a thick forest
lose sight of that ugly tree
or the shack-sized rock.
Simple as urinary relief.

All your compass will remember
is the magnetic north.
Not which way the trail is?
Nor where you last saw her?

Had you a compass for a heart,
lostness would be the way of you.

Letter Poem for Joyce

Leaving Lincoln, we climb in an Embraer
a thousand feet over the Platte Valley.
The sun's earliest light reflects from its East
off every lake, pond, and puddle and lights
the dark ground to my opened window.
The other cabin windows all are down.

Ponds, lakes rebut so dry a plain.
Their pilgrim band of light
seems to hold a tracking bearing on us.
A single, moving needle of dawn.

The plane climbs a shelf of bridal tulle
toward our sheets at home.

Mnemosyne Shrugs

First, we talked ourselves
into a neighborhood of two.
Then you and I played tennis.
Then we played other things.
I think I became mean
as I had not quite been; perhaps
that something so wrong seemed so good,
that something so good could be so wrong.

We dealt our share of hurt,
but asked absolution,
but kept on, and would,
still in good's vaguest cloud.

Attribution

To find those old poems
is to find young love between the lines.
Love that had not aged,
though folded long away,
is to hear again a deep-felt song,
to think "how strange"
something in this old ink
is alive as your living arms.

On Your Gift of Gioia's Poetry

To read some of these now,
knowing enough to know
I'd seen some of them before,
but just enough, how wonderful still!
Gioia tells you just enough and has your mind
help with the poetry; the way love works, you
know just what is meant and are flattered
all over again. Yet already at eighty-two,
memory won't hold the individual words so well
as when I could say them in stanzas or tropes
gazing out a tram car glass
on a crowded street in Berlin,
or away from you in any old fit of
                    lostness.

Before the Last Rejection

for Joyce

You read my piece with smiles and tears.
You, my source, my always acceptance.
You, a personification of what form should be.
Who run my meters off the page.
In a loss of counting, back to verse
We once called free. A word so little
Understood in poetry.

Section IV

Reading Our Letters, Last to First

I begin at the bitter end. Heart's Irish pennant.
Where you speak of ambivalent feelings
and how nothing is fun anymore,
how you are sleeping too much,
and read toward the first,
to the place where I tell you how your voice
is music to get me through the day,
then on to where you say my coat of arms
is crayon on old wallpaper or glyphics
I carved in the soft skin of river birches,
bravely making them bleed.
Now I read your finely elliptical reply
to the poem I wrote for you at Christmas,
coming at last to the night we talked
of Greene and Smollet,
and our glasses touched and our cheeks almost,
to end with the very best, that first surreptitious note
when we barely knew each other.

They Said You Telephoned

If I'd not known
just that you had phoned,
I could have had my Friday night
to waste on other dreams.
I could have enjoyed the baseball game
tonight when there was no moon,
nor afterward would I sit alone
writing senseless verses,
leaving blank spaces for your name.

Morpheus hugs himself
and wants to go to sleep,
perchance to dream of drag bunts
and cloudy slides at second.

See, there was this woman
on the bleacher I was on, who,
from a certain angle,
as she moved to comb
her chestnut hair, said you are alone.
And a freshness in the air
had the memory of October
and a poem I started then
that lacks a final line.

Bob Gaskin

The outfield wears the green
of linen under surgical lights.
A bat cracks, and I mutely stand,
watching a colorful blur
of nameless runners clapping their hands,
rounding bases.
A line forms as they score.

The plate,
home,
the only way to alone.

Van Goes by Dairy Queen

Pastel morning clouds.
October is coming.
A harried motorist assails
me with his horn,
crossing to Kroger's lot.
Another sip of black coffee
someone made early at Dairy Queen.

I ponder quitting as I do
on days like this. I smell
October coming. And I'm slow
in the way of a world that little cares
if the sky is blue, that does not see
the wings of the morning, or
that there is enough
not to speed to, of coffee, a tale,
and someone young to tell it to.

Last Camp

High among the last of the aspens,
near the flume of an abandoned mine,
I fill a pot with icy water,
get some on my hands and feel it
to the arches of my feet. There is no source
of warmth we didn't bring.

The names of skimpy towns
or the site of a single shack,
Purgatory, Crazy-Woman Creek,
tell how these mountains seemed
to those who worked these claims
or came to trap and could not
extricate themselves.

The friends I came with leave to climb,
their pitons and carabiners
clanking up the trail.
I stay in camp, read, wash some things.
Heat water in my tin cup,
making the flame glow orange,
then yellow, then blue.
City lights in December.

Dysthymia

The best about my shapely white candle,
upright in its pewter holder, is
the softness of its light: modest, my flickering,
tentative contender against the night.

Then one thump brings an Irish pennant
to face the day, the sad scent of cooling wax,
hardening to white, in its frozen masquerade,
ice on a backyard water pipe.

Matched, my hand hath torched a light.
Ah, what an element is that.

Träumerei

Fingertip nights. The summer moon,
the room bereft of all
but its soft light. Your belly
is moondust, undulant,
my undaunted dream. Such nights
unhallow, unwean the world.
The ballpark when the club's away,
me sliding home in the dark.
Easy, you say.

Morning. Dream woman you are
gone. Sleep's consciousness
squints back the raucous lies
of overrated day.

Breakfast alone, Armenian
at the Jerome. Melon,
slices of orange, eggs, and tea,
lines by Marvel, a gong and tapestries,
music, classical, to eat by.
You would love it here.
So would I.

Devices

A paper page, one that I can bend,
Sideline, underline, and annotate,
Dog-ear, hold in my warm hand,
Smelling of paper, leather, no acetate
Or other chemical, no snap-in batteries,
Or wire; a thing my paperweight rock
From Mauthausen would batter. I mean
Its thin, narrow, tinselly death-like screen.
A Kindle is to a book as an email is to a letter,
Quickly sent, quickly read, forgotten even faster.

While I Wait

I dread enough the thought,
All the more the genesis of it.
How I could miss the ting of a kitchen pot
Or the rattle of bread pans on their racks.

What thought?

That I'll be as morose as I ought:
Void of essence, the true and forever absence.
No miracle of your coming in the door at 2 a.m.
No dropped pot on a hardwood floor, no secret song.

No being waited on, only waiting,
A found line lost on a new poem
Or you lightly saying, "I'm going now."

Last Paper Book, 2084

Set me like a sarcophagus
upright in your display glass
that shoppers strolling down the century,
phones to ear, might pause,
come turn a paper page, and see
how in a green tree this was done.
Bookman stand a bier for me.

Used Readers

Readability is guaranteed,
or your interest returned
for a choice of something else.
Some of these are rescues.
All have earned their place,
nods the octogenarian seller.

Maybe some have been in jail,
none stink of a garbage bin.
You hold one, bend it,
feel the printed pages turn.
Lift it from its parent wood.
Mark an opus with a line.

Yet age says it's time. No real
buyers. Best offer is three K,
to haul them out, don't need
the books. Empty, clean up.
No hint that ghosts
walked here once.

Western Ways

Six or so old paperback westerns?
You think your undercount cost us twenty dollars?
You shame yourself wrongly. No money left the
cash box. Six old books of the least quality
left our shelves, just paper, whose material
worth can be but pennies.

Yet you brush more powder off your wings.
My blasts do worse, almost any day.
It's not the paper, of course. One cannot weigh,
cannot in all science quantify the ideal,
the dreams, the hopes, the fantasies inky old pulp
might resuscitate or satisfy. Cowboys don't cry,

certainly, you shouldn't. Worn-out men may need
their armchair savagery perfumed in cordite
and spin their cylinders in their minds, one
in six (about the same odds as being seventy-nine).
Just let them limp on off, their waddage spent
years ago in some good season.

Insight Before a Slow Computer

In this world of faults and failures,
it was my own ineptitude I laid it to.
No long-awaited photograph illumed my screen,
no sweet face
nor memory of innocence
such as I, too, once held in both hands.
No. Just a blinking cookie waving to a dunce
baffled by an array of blinking possibilities.

I've done it wrong so many times before
it was the part of reason to assume the fault were mine.

Ah, but today the answer comes,
and my too-often cursed machine
brandishes in my face a delight to please a man
who thought himself a poet once,
with this message, "God made all things beautiful,"
the baby's eyes in which one sees oneself,
its mother's hand, a mother's hands.

Men can only try, make a poem here,
there a painting of the elderly finger of God,
or a tower that reaches halfway to the sky.
Still men will try.

Section V

The Custodians

Saints once walked here.
That is as clear
as a cold night full of stars.

A nail in a hooligan's rundown heel
scalks the concrete walk.
Dostoevsky was always clear enough.

For its fastidious restraints,
Owen turned away from poetry and became
a poet, and we could all go straight to hell;

and Yeats sat clanging the dinner bell,
dreaming of Byzantium and purity.
Pounds of pigment came. More's the pity.

Some idiot, you see, keeps breaking up the porcelain.
They've nailed the fences to growing and dying trees.
They season now your porridge just any way they please.

Homage to Egil Skallagrímsson

It's nights when they've done it again
that I am Egil. And the eyes grow distant
and glassy, and human factors are so much crap.
It's when they've failed utterly and the moon
grows heavy that I more than see Egil's point.

No, their helmets bore no horns. Adornments.
Fit for the ribboned warriors of later centuries,
for Kirk Douglas, oar-hopper *par excellence*.
And I bend my fist around the cup,
read its Rune, its heart-light chill.
Evil is Egil.

As my hair flies wild and I pound the table,
I concur. Winners all are Egil. This sooth
must be glossed over with courtesies, but
you know when the greetings, solicitous inquiries,
and soft hands and fond adieus
hide the rough heart of Egil.

This is the truth, so listen well.
You'll hear it nowhere else. Egil runs the world.
To be civilized is with grace to out-Egil Egil,
the Man of La Mancha notwithstanding
(as of course he wasn't or didn't).
Tonight I side with Egil.

Bob Gaskin

All the world is ill. I sit, play it over,
no simpering, nostalgic Bogey, hearing soft music.
Let my slain enemies rot in the corner
among the fish and otter bones. Drink, fear not,
the night raiders' mist will insulate your heart,
as it did Egil's.

The wintry wind is kinder still than they,
I shudder in the embrace of that moaning lover.
The smudge lamp swings in the strongbacks.
The compass floats in its icy bowl.
The dark reveals its secret pilot star to you
if you are Egil.

Thinking Low

Ah yes, Macbeth hath murdered sleep
And Birnam Wood is on the march
For Dunsinane. The lady hath proved
her mettle as Genesis foreshadowed.
Something wicked this way comes,
The book, the prophets, and witches
So soothly foretold.

Still, Macbeth had been a better thane
To have sipped from his tankard and dreamed
By his fire, leaving his portcullis up.
He might have worn laurels on his head,
Not done what the witches knew he would.

The Bard

Young, I read him for his pretty tropes.
The berries on the bush were quite enough,
As if the mink from its metal trough
Catalyzed a mash-fed world to softly stroke
A grand-dame's inherited neck.

Aged now, I see those queries left opaque,
Hamlet, Lear, and Macbeth, and gladly awake
To only night's murders to wrestle with.

Wilfred Owen

Beyond criticism,
his moving eye found art
where no art lived, nor little else
but contrasts,
like seabirds, white
against the darkest sky,
as flares and gas shells
are lovely in their way
above the snaked-out graves
and treeless mire
of no man's land.

Homage for Lieutenant Owen

He paused and looked at the sky
without speaking, as if he were lost in a dream
of green fields long ago; the way an eye
looked sadly once on murderous Jerusalem,
forgiving everything, everyone.
One must advance down death's bank toward home.

What if, instead, Yeats had smelled the rank wind
off these November muds, or bound young dreams
in a sodden wad for grave details to find,
or slept in a frog spawn he had only seen
and died too soon, before he'd half begun
to write a doctored dotage out in poems
on what a protracted life can do to one
of the fire-side anguish of impotent old men?

Enigma

What could be more shocking than to see
Friends' bodies shattered in war? For some,
Such visions are indelible defilers of sleep.
But then to hunt and shoot animals for fun?
Does this not pose a psychological conundrum,
With a gun, to shoot a harmless thing alive,
See its terrified eyes cloud to opaque,
Show it to an admiring someone, for what sake?

Looking for Work at Middle Age

He hangs like a furred "H" clutching two power lines,
the squirrel. The current flowing through his corpse
for days, judging from the bloat and the flies
Unused to finding anything dead so far from ground.

But why are the swarming flies not killed? A
larval insult to being. Perhaps the answer lies
in polarities. Someone would know. Is not
the east now a raw wire such as grackles stand on?

Those powdery paws clutch four fists of instant
death, the power that lit my screen last night
as Hamlet bemoaned life's snares and the Bengal's
field goal from thirty yards out split his upright spine.

A siren approaches from the children's channel.
A blue arc leaps from his stiff hair to a stick
I throw. He must stay till linemen come
or time dries him like a leaf for the last fall,

Though it puts a different flavor in my coffee,
his just hanging there, an "H" that won't drop
over the patio where I've brought down squadrons
in my sleep and got a ticket once for burning limbs.

On these forms, there is no blank for what's important.
I should know who to call.

From Chagall's *Lovers in Venice*

Before a backdrop sun, warm as disease,
two lovers conspire. The picked flowers
he holds obscure her naked breasts.
A lone scraggy goat on a hill
dominates the distance beyond the town;
its size would suit the foreground.

The mid-distant city gets short shrift.
A few brushstrokes outline its roofs,
wall, and, in the center, a tower or minaret.
For all it signifies, it could be Samarkand
or a red dirt village in East Texas, any place
that lovers have turned their backs on.

Her look tells it all, head slightly atilt,
watching his response like a pre-dawn druid
awaiting sunrise. One face, crowned now
with daylight, is all she sees.
The goat may care where Venice is.

On Viewing De Andrea's Sculpture in Vienna

Stand quite close and blur your focus a bit
And you will see. De Andrea knew what he was doing
Placing nature against Byzantium. Stand this close,
Then tell me he was not right. Every exact hair her human
Rawness bespeaks, every cast-set labial detail as it was.
You know this woman stood here once just as she is,
And this is as close as you can get. Eat out your heart,
Then tell me again what art is for under the trench coat
Of aesthetics. Stand where De Andrea did
As she looks up in this now frozen stance.
Go ahead, six inches from a kiss, tell me you don't see,
Moles and all, how she exceeds your everything,
Your red wheelbarrow, your bird on its golden limb.

While You Were Away

Tonight, it came to me, on opening
Heaney by the green desk lamp,
that I was reading for nothing now.
Wright's hopeless Judas holding a beaten man.

I was reading Heaney just for him,
lonely and at home, a hard-won freedom
not owed to anyone, no paper due,
no faculty status to be won.

Tell me a litany now on empathy,
on pure poetry. No, rather don't.
The bookshelves fade outside the lamp's
bright cone. I get it. After all those

silly years, heart's Irish pennant has
now a home. To read as when I was a child,
and it's enough to bask in feelings such
as those wordless ones no one understood.

Window Dressing

for Joyce
New Year's Day 2017

The drizzle picks up again, becomes rain.
A grackle perched on a bare and topmost limb
Says, "Damn it," and dives down again
To where a surviving leaf is sure to remain
And shelter him. The grackle thinks it's by plan.
Or is this loneliness, the recurring tautology?

Seven high-flying buzzards slowly circle.
Each in its separate orbit as if an atomic nucleus
Bound them. Can they see something dead
Five hundred feet below? Or has the wind
Compounded an attractive ball of scent,
Incentive to the ugliest of birds and my poem?

They seem content effortlessly to drift
In a drunk rook's rondelet past my view of sky.
Oh, will they all, new leaves, new grackles,
Buzzards too, be born and die again, over
And over as Nietzsche said they would?
Packaged in eons or each by ignorant each?

Lies *for* Morning

Would you live and come again? Or I? Are we
As mad as Nietzsche was to think we would?
Surrounded by our shop's twelve thousand books,
I sit, puzzling outside our glass at a lone sparrow
On Mai's shop's shingle across the way as I do each
Day save Sunday when we hear another story.

Figures of Speech

The Wonderfulest Dad in the World
Stands with his plastic face to the wall
In the single BR's closet, in the semi-hall,
Discreetly now unseen,
For when the children come,
Among the half-woven
Tapestry wedding gift
From friends in Guatemala.
And files of promises we said,
other ironies that were told for true
in their time. With our lens,
We can, in time, explain.

Let me now guess what a lens for:
In the Hubble, the eye of a crow,
Your telephone, a Tarzan beetle
In the grass? It's a translator
Through the diverse optics of its spectrum,
Reveals and shields your world.
I walk to my car, eyes dilated.
Is this then the untranslated true state,
This now blinding light?
My horse in darkness could track
The thickest trails. I'd lean on his neck.
My cat says night is a truer reality.

Lies *for* Morning

"Could you slam your door on him again?
Why aren't you happy?" the ghost of Wilder
Asks Housman's ghost as they, in their separate boats,
Shove off to hell. "Why? After you wrote those poems?"
Such a line the Bard could have asked himself
As he turned his ink-marked hand to real estate
And left us to ourselves? Or was he prescient
Enough to know that our noblesse would deny him?

Substitute Teaching at Seventy

At last, I know what Miss Kopke knew
Who said she didn't know
What we were coming to.
We too would teach "The Road Not Taken,"
We who came by the one that is.
Over the transom, the sky is still Van Gogh's.

After Midnight Mass

Leaving in the night, you know something passes.
True love's season ended again, moved on, evaporated
Like summer rain on grass, night's lost its song.
Tomorrow, the returns begin, the tabulating
Of receipts, of clothes that would have
Kept Him warm, guns, galoshes, a dress all wrong
For her, his pant size too optimistic for a year.
A remnant hovers like smoke from a dead fire,
Music, reminding busy clerks and shoppers of the
Never ending always flowing never adequate want of love,
The tidying up of harvest home as winter comes.

Group Dynamics

Did Ms. Wordsworth leave him a poet home
And go to meet with motley friends?
None of whom would know a count
From an uncount noun? Was it that
Together they would discern deep and inner
Things in books. Or was it that it was so like
What she had done in another life? They
Could be together then and read in turn.
They'd share two hours free from separate
Homes, where all that could possibly be
Already had been done.
                    But still hags and crones
Can dream, even half redress old wrong, as
She once fancied listening at home to him.

Delmore[2]

        I read your book
of daemons and find myself wishing
that you still lived, that I
could send you something—not literary
praise, but something you still could use,
some money, some worth, some of the common
validation of this earth.

On a park bench among the litter
of Washington Square you sit, one shoe untied,
the stub of a cigarette in your grimy hand.
Your hungry, sensitive eyes look askance,
as from barren Parnassus
you survey this contemptible world.
Beneath your bench, a tabloid headline screams,
"HEIRESS TO KEEP HER MILLIONS," as if a truth
came tumbling like a dead, dry desert bush
to lodge by you, wadded, wind-blown,
came screaming that lurid paean—
Mother America's final word.

---

[2] Atlas, James. 2020. *Delmore Schwartz : The Life of an American Poet*. New York Farrar, Straus And Giroux, p.180–181.

Section VI

Forces That Never Give In

A shard of sharp rock came down the dawn
with the last ice age.
It crossed in a morning with ancient men,
over the Bering Strait on a pink ice bridge.
Yesterday, it flatted my steel-belted Michelin
at a most inopportune point in geologic time.

I watched a grimy man dig it out
with a pocketknife. In the near dark, I saw
him flense something wet from the raw
underside of a bloody flap of mastodon skin.
He tossed the stone out on the pebbled ground,
thoughtlessly back into the flow of years.

Someone will get the point again.
There are forces that never give in.

Primal Sympathy

Sweeping down off the polar crust,
Boreas, in the dawn of lust,
Saw the old primordial sea
Change to blood and quicken thee.

The coagulating cold of birth
Shrank into greener earth;
Stooping creatures, becoming upright,
Dominated all in sight.

Gods were dreamed by orphan men,
Gods could lead them home again,
And teachers declared with sacred text
One saint a heathen to the next.

Hindus and Buddhists cannot please us
Who napalmed hovels for sweet Jesus,
For we have eaten holy bread
Where Woden's boyish prayers are said.

Who broke the crypts of Tutankhamen?
Saffroned beggars? Some naked Brahmin?
Go search, in the Paleolithic ice,
The ashes of man's first sacrifice,

Bob Gaskin

Where shadows of crouching cannibals
Flickered on the frozen walls—
Millennia before we came
With purer fire, in honor's name.

Hearing the Language

Maybe it was an opossum talked to me
Last night. No nightingale ever did.
Neither has an anthropomorphic god,
Not by sign, nor any *lingua* known to me,

But last night the wind was up, and I saw it,
What seemed to be a torn flap of canvas
In the street. But it was dark ,and I was late.
The semi-edge of gray-brown cloth lifted
And fell back as a tent's groundsheet might
When not securely tabbed against a wind.

Coming home by the same neighborhood street,
I saw it had a face, possum-ugly, rat-like
To the un-cute tail. It still was pushing
Its fore half up; the rest was crushed to paste.
Its jaws were opening and closing as if
Trying to plead in possum tongue or shriek.

I did a U-turn and came back, then stopped,
Leaned out and placed the left front tire just right.
I felt the crunch and a tiny sound,
A finger drawn quickly down clean glass.
First light, I shoveled it into a clean box.
It seemed the thing, not to leave it there, as if
It had been calling, like to some deity.

Tsunami

It was to them like Armageddon came,
and the rainbow was one more lie.
God killed the mother, the father, and the son,
then drew out like a rapist
when he's done. We
won't eat his fishes now, swirled
from the dirty sink where Dante's
demons chew upon the damned.

Who will come to surf the human flotsam
or grow numinous now when sunset comes
or make a poem here where nature mocked
her paragon all one day? Call not the sea
your mother, not those rank and fickle depths
you left when time began, crawled up upon
purgation's blood-warm shore, struggling to become
what she can't forgive.

Peacocks

Fan-feathered, they promenade
Past my therapist's bay window.
Why, I ask, such display?
"To get more peacock," he replies,
"Or make others think they do."
Do they so fancy those garish colors?
"Yes. But size also matters. Observe
Our puffed-up pigeons every spring."
Astonishing. Wouldn't the species
Select itself larger and larger with time?
"Some say size matters only to males.
This sameness suggests an affirmation."
Do peacocks fly? "Do peacocks fly!
One was sitting on either side of me
From Vienna to Houston yesterday."

"Do I detect a touch of doubt?
Visit any men's locker room.
Observe as they pass from
Dress, to nude, to kit; then
An hour later, must do it back,
Dual metaphases of revelation.
Hark how language becomes puffed up
In blank chorus of birdlike chirp,
In an ego ping pong played by tongue
Instead of loud and hollow balls."

Lunchbox Gen

"Oil refinery? Was it hazardous then?"
Heated oil is very fractious. That's its value:
gases, gasoline, asphalt, down to bunker crude.
Not like water, everything off at two-twelve.
And water vapor is not flammable.
Ground fog turned to fire one morning.

"Any fatalities in your time there?"
On the job? Nineteen in thirty-three years.
Seven were killed one worst Monday.
Burns can fool you, but all died in two weeks.

"Any of them friends?"
Oh yeah, two, one close. Stainless died last,
both instrument men. They're often present
where control problems are building.

"How could you go back next day?"
Put two tuna sandwiches in a lunchbox,
chips, a cookie, a coverless Shakespeare.
Try to forget yesterday's snake-skin cloud.
God, I could have followed it there.
But the next day was reins on the neck.
The Ford knew the way, like old Powder
on night trails you didn't need to see.

Spring Planting

Probably a hundred fifty, two hundred spade fulls,
each pushed down flush into the soft earth,
are enough to turn up this plot. Easy.
The guy who lived here hauled in soil
and planted, judging from the humus
and the healthy worms, probably twice a year.

Good therapy, they say,
to dig in the dirt. Put seeds in and sticks
for crawlers. They say watching things grow,
especially what you plant and tend yourself, helps. They say
sleeping with bread quiets the dreams of the starved.
One thing sure, short of late freeze or a stupid

mistake with the fertilizer, I'll have a garden,
my *götterdämmerung* over this insect's fiefdom.
The shovel slips in with just the right resistance.
Easy, it hardly tugs as I lift, turn over the earth.

Amateur

"A man does better to stay with what he knows,"
my all-too-candid mechanic mumbled, re-threading
the spark plug hole that I had stripped.

"A man needs to know his limitations,"
Dirty Harry mused, after the crooked cop
had exceeded his. This I recalled sliding off her roof:

A bathroom vent stopped my fall, then I was
Gaston Rébuffat self-arresting on the Jungfrau,
Saint Francis offering help, however pointless,

Or Dodo Delwin, Skelton's clown, showing how
to fall or be a fool so that all but the angels laugh.
In my room, two diplomas hang from tiny nails.

O'Hanlon once taught the wrong century.
One day, a San Juan guide stepped on the wrong rock.
We saw the chopper as we were starting up.

Planting a garden at Rehab. It's a start.
The shovel slips in with only slight resistance.
All one does is lift, turn over the earth.

To Dirt Returneth

If the piers are tall enough, a play town
can be built beneath a house;
ours had roads of smoothly patted dirt,
each carefully curbed with talcum earth,
slightly moist in the dank cool of the house.
Bridges linked hummocks, and hills made
natural valley—natural to our dirt town,
for they were there before we came,
turned up perhaps by workmen long ago—
but now we made dam in them
and let the brimming lake threaten the city
and cast over our creation a subtle dread.
The secret is to not fill the sump so full
that the water breaks the thinner upper dam,
but never not fill full enough,
for then there'd be no worry in the town.
And we had minarets in our broad culture,
and an airport should never be downtown,
but that's where ours was;
the ceiling was constantly two and a half feet
(our childish world had absolutes),
but movement was free enough
so long as we either sat or crawled
to push the play cars through the streets.

Bob Gaskin

That summer saw the very hand
Which patted a play world in the sand,
Smash the dam and loose a flood
And bomb with clods the neighborhood;
And ripping and kicking through earthen homes
We bashed in Samarkand's sacred domes.
The city was scattered, returned to dirt;
But friend, our raid did nobody hurt.
We just grew bored with the careful plan,
And somewhere in boredom lurked archetypal man.

Earthquake

Suddenly, nothing is fixed.
Benchmarks rise and sink.
The parking lot has waves.

The whole town wobbles like its alcoholics.
The true drunk barely notices
concentric circles in his drink.
(What's one more passing shudder?)

A few bricks fall.
A horn blows in an empty car.

Two die, neither communist
nor gay. An Act of God?
The ground slipped to no conclusion.
The great fault moved is all.

If only this were not so familiar,
the world threatening to shake itself apart,
a dark form waiting in another room,
and mother won't have a word.

No wall you make is safe.

Nightmare

In a dream, I deliberately killed a fluffy cat
By spraying it with something vile and green.
Sleepless, I sank in the library chair and sat
Unable to disbelieve I'd done the thing.

Again, another negating homunculus
Though my cat, Monty, sleeps half on me in bed,
Whom I'd mourn grievously if he were dead.
He'd come a haggard starveling up to us.

I'll tell such haunts, "It's you again."
Monty will tell you I took him in.
And he I.

April's Way

Near 80, I get what Eliot meant by cruel.
An ice cream truck's fake calliope
pumps out spring's early "Te Deum" again.

A song of children, and of the sweets
I'd buy for them, father in a world
whose pain, as always, must be learned.

I case the ancient ice cream man,
see his hoary arm disappear
again and again into a cloud of frost,

and how as he digs, chill bumps form
on a tattooed heart with a woman's name,
under winter camouflage.

One more season's leaves are down.
With little taste left for sweets,
I jettison my useless change
into his cup and, too, go on.

Art and Its Place

Young Adolf's admissions professors
found his sense of perspective wanting.
And, rejecting him, showed scant feeling
for what the art world lost. Were they so old,
so enamored of rule and plan, archaic
keepers of the boundaries of this world?

They might have guided him on
to be a common Rankian half-neurotic,
and thus have earned credit for creating
the most serious Dadaist in the world.
Who like half-artists, they the world over
found less destructive uses for their hate.

Pour Me Another

A less-than-ant-size infant bug
Travels a line, as if to my shoe.
Has it a concept analogous to fear?
I tap my foot, blocking its path.
Yet it comes on, only avoiding destruction
By my moving my shoe. No fear?
What senses or their lack guide it?

As the well frog's universe is cylindrical,
Snake, to reed, to oaken bucket,
Can the bug not see in two dimensions?
Does it not see at all? Scampering
Steadily, as if any space bettered another?
What need, dare I say wish, drives it into my sole?
Substances in a bug-killer's cloud may explain.

Prayer Patch for an Octogenarian

At eighty, one does such things, I'd read,
To make youth shudder at what's ahead.
Like my grandson married one full year
Before I was privileged actually to meet HER.
Her name, Anna, I'd mistaken for Mary.
I confess I called her Mary in my prayers.
But what, then, did God hear?

"Even in prayer, your foul-ups are revelation,"
My Roman Catholic priest-friend sighed.
"But good enough. Most of us prayed to her.
Son, He knows your heart, as well as your error.
Bless you. But read again the Roman letter."

Section VII

Sparrow Psalm

A sparrow trapped inside the sun porch
tries and tries, again and again, to fly
through the unforgiving screen.
It drops to the deck for a half rest.
The beat of its despairing heart is visible.
I open the outside door to the yard
and then must frighten it to freedom.
This has happened before. I exult in this,
to watch it dart wildly into the free sky.
One may not by analogy anoint oneself.
Still, I cannot help but think of Him
Who knows the poor creatures one by one.

Wonder

Tired of the keys, I turn in my chair.
It's early. Can you put in a poem
that you wake up depressed every dawn?
No. No real subject. Just scared of the day.
Of what, you cannot say. Last week,
some TV guy puffed his book that proves
a god just isn't necessary. They've explained
how universes can just happen.
I, turn aside, sip my coffee
and scan the spines of our books—*Gone with
the Wind, Holy Bible, Sophie Scholl, The Complete
Stories of Flannery O'Connor,* Eudora Welty,
and *The Cave,* Hemingway—*A Moveable Feast.*
But who can explain depression anyway, except
that it just happens, like tiny stones I took from
camps in Germany. One cannot think them part
of a plan. The coffee drained. I must face the day,
Sick in love with what uncreated humans say.
Could we then be creators? Or is that heresy?
Or is it that we only wonder, wonder still what love is?

After the Ovens and Palaces

We found Dietrich's attic room
up two flights to a bare plank floor
and the single bed he slept on.
We wishing he knew we were there,
beside his writing desk and wooden chair,
looking across roofs and chimney pots,
traitors to hate and glory, breathing a free man's air.

His wall was bereft of plaques or guidons,
no Michael posturing with his sword.
Two banks of books on hand-nailed shelves.
Was it here they barked his name? In tones
comedians still mock? No, next door.
They led him off into the dark valley,
afraid their world might end.

In a Holy Rain

"One is as good as what one loves," a burgher
Whispered to Dr. Goebbels, listening to Beethoven
In bombed-out Berlin. Brave trumpets
And drums stirred the rapt audience.
Schiller, the "Joy;" perhaps half tears,
For Mahler's *Kindertotenlieder*.

What voices these shattered ceilings heard,
Applause now shivering fractured glass.
Where cellos and bassoon reclaim
The distant hum of approaching planes.
"Dietrich preached here once," the burgher breathed.
"But, of course, we didn't hear him."

Better Things to Do

In Shorer's photo of the book fires in Berlin,
five brownshirt gatherers descend, steps,
heavily laden with volumes to burn.
It's daylight still; there's dampness on the stone.

The soldiers, aware of Shorer's camera,
exaggerate their loads, backs bent
against the heft of Schiller, Heine, the Grimms.
Remove the poison, a better world will come.

A Hausfrau who'd not lie for a coin
hurries up, proud she's found another book to burn.
She fancies a smiling führer looking down.
Her non-redacted Nietzsche for the fatherland:

Wir waren einst das Volk von Dichter und Denker.
Nun haben wir bessere zu tun als zu denken,[3]
he'd said. They strut on water to the fire.
As drums count cadence, the tiniest match will do.

---

[3] We were a people of writers and thinkers.
Now we have better things to do than to think.

Die Eiserne Jungfrau

They stand the prisoner in an iron sarcophagus,
close the front halves to fasten at the midline.
Sharp spikes hold the condemned upright, unable to sit,
to fully stand, or make a holy sign to her.
By rights, he killed himself. Claustrophobic panic,
self-torn carotids, or a final collapse into the spikes.

No rope, no axe, nor executioner required
for sharpened tines furtive as an alley knife.
A rag picker able to fasten a lock would do;
able to rise from time to time and, bending down,
listen for feet shuffling in their blood.
Then mop the pinkish muck and go home.

Even now, some claim she was ever a virgin,
so strong a deterrent was her abstract terror.
Who could have dreamt a horror more detergent?
Gentler minds thought the poetry might do,
the doomed and hopeless pleading to the *Jungfrau*.
I could not ascend to the third and final floor.

Moses from the High Ground

When God told me to stay up here
and sent the pike men down
with orders not to spare a living soul,
I hoped He thought it wasn't my kind of job.

My once and forever sentence remains to watch.
Is this my mark, as in a one-act plot,
in which no actor moves again?
You wrote my role, and all is done.

My truths are fixed into a mosaic (no pun)
forever. In a green tree, they yet read
how Judas fashioned the faith's first
slip knot. He ties his too over and over.

Fantasia for Maundy Thursday

One could already sense the morbidity.
As if oneself had got it wrong.
It's in the organ's slow clink of nails
On a cold night on a dirty hill.

You could flee if the wind came up
Or rain drove in, find yourself a fire
Where strangers stand, say you are cold.
Say you are not one of them.

Hardly a word would be required
Not here. Not in the faculty lounge,
Even your accent respected.
No pain, no nails. A pot of coffee,
A table round, and half an hour to kill.

Alypius in the Coliseum

At the crowd's roar, rising wave over wave,
crescendoing through the Coliseum's arches,
he just had to open his eyes. He would not,
he'd sworn to his friends, for he knew
it was wrong, men hacking each other to death
for the blood lust of Caesar's, the cruelty
okayed from on high, approved by the finest
ladies of the empire. No one had to come.
You could always choose another channel.

But his innards vibrated. The crowd controlled
his decent heart. His eyes were opened.
Could they all be wrong? Could this feeling,
not unlike the Holy Spirit, be denied?
Don't we know death itself can be overcome?
And fear, pain? Common daily to every man.
Now he would drag his friends to this new thing.
"You must come too," he would have said to Augustine.

Dust and Ashes

Bellarmine knew the earth was properly centered,
heaven's focus, bright blue-green haven
set in a cloud of stars. Damned he, Galileo,
whose glass, charts, and numbers demurred.
All these ages, illiterate serfs who never heard
of such men toiled in God's grace, their every
unschooled word lost with them in the dust
they tilled, their muddy boots beside the door
a better cross than Bellarmine's brocaded arms
lifting the sacred presence to.

Consider the holy fires, old heretics burning the new
in Jesus' name, Jesus who wept. They search
old ashes of those fires, journalists of a paper god,
declare new paradigms, new ways to play.
An infant birthed by candle in a vermined shed,
lifted by gnarled and calloused hands onto
the belly of His love, screams truer prayers,
a supplication no humane-divine need interpret.
Love does not come into the world again.
Only the need for it. Your guilty hand is the body
of the Lord. You fed his children with your human blood.

Absurd

Tonight, we slammed our door on him.
Even Peter ran, Peter the saint,
Choking in terror, denying his friend.
Is this life absurd? Of course it is.
Is life worth it, nevertheless?
Its sorrows, rumors, and rotting death?
Only one who bore our worst
Could answer this.

Creation

Into a sound pattern I did not make,
It's as if she takes my mind as mother did
My hand, showing a magic rhythmical way
By water's edge, half on sand, half on the brew
Of eternity. There is a metric to this I cannot spring,
An angel in a Wenders film, and thumpings by which
Atoms were made out of nothing, or so
It seems. Mnemosyne lies with me in dreams.

Todesangst

The fear is worse than the fact,
the latter universal to humankind.
Yet, who does not dread to leave
love that soon must let you go?
What known paradise would call you
in permanence away from all
that human love can take and give?
Through a one-way door marked love
from which no traveller returns,
to that place of dreams, dreams
of what? Your dear one's lips,
her ineffable transport into the divine,
our back and forth in time, to a timeless heaven?

Don't Ask

When memory leaves like white rain
And our lion is a kitty in the zoo,
Could we make human love again?
Would you be like someone new?
Does Van Gogh hug his lover in the hay?
Does love live on that way?
Is that what is meant by art and pain?

Cold Island

There is a cold island.
On it, I've pitched my tent.
He who comes and taps my pot
out here will be cold too.

Let him not judge my secret
source of warmth, nor say
how acrid is its taste,
snug with his coat of down

and stacks of tropical brochures.
The wind that stabs his civil heart
strikes no pain in mine.
Let him not curse my bitter wine.

The Door

Don't close that door.
It's a door you can never
open again. Not even with
apologies and tears.
You'd be forever the closer.
Use a hammer, even a chisel.
Marvel, it might budge, even
go crashing down. The open wall
will never let you in again.

Section VIII

Lies and Paper Angles

Margie and I were playing on my family's porch.
She, about five, was teaching me to do cutouts.
At about four, I knew lies were wrong, clearly
As Eden's apples and little George's cherry tree.

This very morning, Mother appeared in the screen
With a simple question, a tiny nothing, long forgotten.
All I remember is that my answer was a lie,
And that the color of the sky did not change.

Mother's acceptance was inconsequential,
But formed my discovery of a new use for words.
Margie didn't notice. She was teaching me
How to cut proper angles in the doll paper.

"No, no. You cut two lines to meet in a corner.
Don't try to curve one line the way you do."
You'd think, in the waste, they'd be gone forever,
Mom sunken into the screen forever;
Margie, scraps and scissors in her hands.

Night and Day

Were I one-bit musical,
I'd try this as a song,
soft words in angel's tongue.
A tune to say Pain itself moves on.

I'd praise the way one soft hand
out-wrests the demon's arm,
false Kantor of fragile reason,
mourner of the day star's coming.

Are you known by a secret name?
You of the on and on. Do you not have
a better home? No lexicon for complaint,
safe where angels feel no pain?

Gerade Aus

Half a block away,
I shouted a perfect
direction change:

"Gerade aus!" Four
compact syllables,
and those men waved,

then turned into the alley
they sought. But twice,
with more bombast:

"Gerade aus, dann links,"
and they turned happily left on
my publication in Heidelberg.

Art's Weakness

The most loving poem
I ever printed for her
was not quite true.

The action, a folded flower,
never grew to picking up.
Only the feeling existed

in the lines,
not quite
lies. No, not lies.

Letter to My Kinder

Just past the clockhouse is a building of cinder
blocks. The sky is very dark and threatening to storm
this morning. I work in the cinder block house.
On the street between here and the clockhouse,
amber pebbles are embedded in the asphalt, sunk
where they were poured years before I came.
They seem to glow in the strange light
this morning as I cross them, passing
in my twenty-first gray February here. They are
like fossils on the old and crusted shore
of an early Cambrian sea. The rust on the
metal windows is emitting gold and blood
and starlight from some midnight escarpment.
The sky is a dead fish. It will change
and be the same. All timecards lie.
There is little I can say. I am old.
I have the feeling all has been told.

After a Friend's Posthumous Anniversary

If I should die before you do
And have to leave my angel here,
I'd ask to camp by God's great door
To see your eyes awaked there.

Midnight Ghosts

an existential chant

Night's car-sized turbine rolls.
It whines, in ascending RPMs,
That old ex-siren song. Oh lumens,
Humming the plant's one-tone procession.
Then the dark mass of morning returns,

Goes back to an elevated's passing
Rattle of a last night dying.
No goodbyes, no lies for mourning.
As a streetlamp's violet moon
Half-lights the mist-damp flagstone.
In and out bands are for Movietone.
Who would come at 5 a.m.,
But the waiting cab waits, its door open.
My glove clears a receding view,
confirming that she watches until
we turn toward earth's widest sea.

Go Your Way and Tell No One

She sat herself up on one arm,
the other reaching to empty air.
She had not been able to do that.
Her focal point unmistakable,
her garbled joy clear beyond words.
I was time's alien and alone.

What would I say to those who come,
jaded to grief's hyperbole?
Would it be truer to say she's dead
or that I'd seen a faint and distant cloud
become a raging army, whipping
its snorting horses down to the sea,
only to find that it had parted?

Last Words

The night she died, I held her up in bed
while the old man spooned the last medicine.
That night, the angels came.
As I held her close, she asked in whispers,
"Have you been drinking?" She had prayed
a thousand prayers that I'd be different,
the hope of her life said a tiny goodbye again.

A lie might have been good. One beer,
I might have said. Amazingly, she raised
to one elbow and spoke to air, eyes
focused to just over the foot of her bed.

"No more now forever," I might have said,
one last painted-over lie. Holy Mary,
Mother of God, I'll make you up,
then try to make up to you.

Deliver Thee from Evil

No, I'll not make a list of my faults
and dispel the items one by one.
I could refute them with little abuse of reason.
Better abstemious prayers. What we have, dear,
is a communications problem,
one with little to do with reason.

But don't throw it out on that account,
or you might topple the universe,
send time curling back into the interstellar dusts
from which, borne on wings of light, it came,
with tolerance uncaring, spinning off saints
and maniacs raging in secret garrets.

So don't do that. You may charge me
with unfairness; I'm its true son. Or say,
since it is true, that deception was my gift
and my soul bent like a sinker ball, low
and outside, sagged like Einstein's everything.
Tell how dust wishes somehow to be dust again.

Get it right. But don't leave out our comfy sphere of pain,
as endless as those circled wagons were,
pure as Vaughan's ring of never-ending light
and lies for morning made up in the night.
Two words can rhyme the ending of a pair:
My metaphysic was crafted to give offense
And lived on the least detectable response.

My Place

Out of place in a place I do not know,
A dream theme all too common comes,
One I am expected to know, and I don't.
The dream director expects me to
remember what I forgot
And whips me with an inch-wide buckled belt.
Confessing what one did not do
Is twice a lie.
Double licks for that.
As mornings denouement,
I shudder awake,
Stagger in to wash my lost face.

Last Whole Earth Song

When the last wild bird has sung
and the last seditious dreamer has dreamt,
when the last great tree has crashed to the ground
and the creatures of earth are asleep,
then you will know how Armageddon came,
that it did not cross in the night while you slept.
Then you can re-read in the ashen rain
what the Scions of Commerce wrote
in the psalter of their pieties where they spoke
like Bishops of the Earth, talked till God grew deaf
and sick of hearing
their blue lips speak his name.

And Now to Close …

The moon bellies down Buddha-like
In the marsh tonight,
And as he does, I say a koan
Silently to him, that on this planet
Spinning out of time,
We kiss pure lovers in our sleep.
And peace is green, quiet
common as grass,
And happiness an animal
Slowly crossing a flowered plain.

About the Author

Bob Gaskin, a native southeast Texan, took early retirement as senior lab technician from Fina Oil Refinery in order to teach English and English as a Second Language at Lamar University where he also later co-directed the Language Institute. He earned a BA in Psychology and an MA in English. As a teen and young adult, before being drafted into the Navy, he rode bulls and helped his father in his income tax agency. He and his first wife raised three children. He backpacked in the mountains, read deeply and broadly, ran (finishing two marathons), made many trips to Germany, and one summer attended a language institute in Vienna to further his German. For some 25 years, he and his wife, Joyce, owned and ran Red B4 Books, a place of good books and lively conversation.

www.ingramcontent.com/pod-product-compliance
Lightning Source LLC
Chambersburg PA
CBHW022108090426
42743CB00008B/759